Goldbeater's Skin

T0164262

Publication of this book was supported by a grant from
The Greenwall Fund of The Academy of American Poets.

The Colorado Prize
for Poetry

Strike Anywhere, by Dean Young
selected by Charles Simic, 1995

Summer Mystagogia, by Bruce Beasley
selected by Charles Wright, 1996

The Thicket Daybreak, by Catherine Webster
selected by Jane Miller, 1997

Palma Cathedral, by Michael White
selected by Mark Strand, 1998

Popular Music, by Stephen Burt
selected by Jorie Graham, 1999

Design, by Sally Keith
selected by Allen Grossman, 2000

A Summer Evening, by Geoffrey Nutter
selected by Jorie Graham, 2001

Chemical Wedding, by Robyn Ewing
selected by Fanny Howe, 2002

Goldbeater's Skin, by G. C. Waldrep
selected by Donald Revell, 2003

Whethering, by Rusty Morrison
selected by Forrest Gander, 2004

Goldbeater's Skin

POEMS BY G. C. WALDREP

Center *for* Literary Publishing
Fort Collins

Set in Centaur.
Printed in the United States of America.
Cover designed by Nicole Hayward.

Library of Congress
Cataloging-in-Publication Data

Waldrep, George Calvin, 1968–
Goldbeater's skin : poems / by G. C. Waldrep.
p. cm. -- (The Colorado prize)
ISBN 1-885635-06-0 (pbk. : alk. paper)
I. Title. II. Series.
PS3623.A358G65 2003
811'.6--dc22
2003020326

The paper used in this book meets the minimum
requirements of the American National Standard
for Information Sciences-Permanence of Paper
for Printed Library Materials, ANSI Z39.48-1984.

2 3 4 5   07 06 05

CONTENTS

ACKNOWLEDGMENTS

Many thanks to the editors of the publications in which these poems first appeared: *American Letters & Commentary, American Literary Review, Arts & Letters, Ascent, Asheville Poetry Review, Barrow Street, Bellingham Review, Black Warrior Review, Blackbird, Conduit, DIAGRAM, Evansville Review, Gettysburg Review, Gulf Coast, Image, Perihelion, Pleiades, Runes: A Review of Poetry, Slope, South Carolina Review, Sycamore Review,* and *Tin House.* "Apocatastasis" first appeared in *Poetry.*

"Elberta" is for Suki Kim, "Nine West Clay" for Mathias Svalina, "Canticle for the Second Sunday in Lent" for Geoff Brock, "Vendible Aesthetic" for Bradley Wester, "In the Gate of Samaria" for Stephanie Saldaña, and "Luminous Bodies" for Rachel Galvin.

Gracious thanks to the Corporation of Yaddo, the MacDowell Colony, the Virginia Center for the Creative Arts, the Vermont Studio Center, the Ucross Foundation, the Robert M. MacNamara Foundation, the Bread Loaf Writers' Conference, and to my parents for assistance during the days in which many of these poems were written. To Donald Revell, for seeing what I see. And to friends whose close readings made this manuscript a better one: Elizabeth Bradfield, Patricia Chao, Kevin Craft, Tony Farrington, Rachel Galvin, Ilya Kaminsky, Karen King-Aribisala, Paul McCormick, Greg Murr, Christine Perrin, Pablo Peschiera, Carl Phillips, Roger Sedarat, Arthur Sze, Jennifer Tonge, Mark Yakich, John Yau, and Dean Young.

Goldbeater's Skin

After this I became more serious. "I can see three things,"
I said. "A game, a scorning, and an earnestness. . . ."

—Julian of Norwich

FATAL EXCEPTION

I do not want *story*. *Story* has had enough.

What happens next is an impossible preposition.
What happens next is where to put the clause.
What happens next is my giving up.
What happens next is frost.

Outside what happens, nasturtiums still blaze.

What happens next is Jonathan.
What happens next is soap.
What happens next is the honeycomb.
What happens next is *(night)*.

Outside what happens belongs to narrative.

What happens next is a strong wind.
What happens next is jail.
What happens next is childbirth.
What happens next is sphere.

Outside what happens, geometry is pure.

What happens next is unthinkable.
What happens next is stylus.
What happens next is distortion.
What happens next is Art.

Outside what happens, sorrow plays coy.

What happens next to Hale-Bopp is falling.
What happens next to wine is meat.
What happens next to carving is *aspen*.
What happens next to *edge* is *park*.

Outside what happens is my own private Arthur.

What happens next is already gone.

I

AGAINST THE MADNESS OF CROWDS

in memoriam Pierre Martory

Reckon the haste of one wall burning.
There is no thickness there is no terror there is
a transparency like oxygen like fire over this bright space.
And will the ashes that rise meet the ashes that fall.
On a light breeze. In this ruined garden.
Is this not physics is this not too much to ask.
This simple question.
For there is a language of flowers as Smart wrote.
There is a language of clouds, and of their wispy orthography
but it is not comforting.
A prayer for a new image, yes:
have we not studied, have we not pasted our rations
in their strict enrollments their proper homologies.
And here, the arrangement of humors.
What I feel in my ribs now is only an echo.
I stand at one distance, I open my wallet
press flesh against cured hide
and I am ready. The blue of the gentian is nothing to me.
The calla, the violet of the iris are nothing
compared to the sky you bring
with your coming when you come with your singing and your sighing
with your counting backward from one hundred
when you come. Is this not too much to ask,
the venation and the marrow
the clandestine order and meaning of all signs.
So while the ashes that rise meet the ashes that fall
I will be the world, for a little while. As such waiting.
The rose of each lung blooms inside.

SYRINX

Walking across the south meadow at evening I see the old snow blue
    like light through leaded windows. Latticed though in fact
    there is no such separation. A sparrow high in the white pine pierces
    with a call that is also like light yet slower

And therefore beneath the range of vision. In addition to the blue note
    there is the red note and the green moving into a lifelike certainty.
    Organic. Seated figure invisible from chin up,

Planes of the body rendered in surplus dimensions; impasto smear.
    Sometimes it is like that, tactile

Without the specificity of impression. A wind moving over the meadow
    like heat falling beneath the surface of breath. The world, touched,
    will return itself to you

According to its original curvature, displacement of affection through
    lack of consciousness rather than desire. Crust on the surface
    where the sun's glare did not quite finish

That old business of sublimation. Therefore dry. Therefore a sky
    clear and cold with stars that make their older music through fire
    as a smith would fashion a length of silver chain, as a glazier

Once fixed tongs on these long panes through which the last rays
    of engagement are growing downward into the roots of things.
    In need of repair I see,

Imperfection seeking its purest array as a perfusion of crystals, a criticism
    of the demotic. Not unworthy. Thinking *absolutely unmixed*
    attention is prayer

Though in fact there is no such separation. Thinking that flight is more
than just an axillary adjustment, still one wants it

More than winged figures, ascending and descending in full view beyond
a silence no less beautiful for all plunder. What else would
they be carrying

Blind as they are. Rungs growing slick-stiff at dusk. Somatic exertion
nothing to them. The received intelligence. Yet if I watch long
enough I will see one stumble.

[IN THE BARROW OF A FORGOTTEN KING]

in the barrow of a forgotten king
I calibrate my hypothesis, this time there will be no mistaking
the orchid for the boy it shields, the boy for the piano,
the piano for the darkness that holds
the way a pair of hands may hold a single dove
and let it go, or not, this is the gilt track that comfort leaves
in its cloud chamber, the illuminated spiral,
I pledged my life's sketch to this experiment, this subdermal insufflation
while the hypnogogue and the hierophant
prattled on, richly robed, I myself knew the limits
of chiasmus, each new life requires mastery
of an additional tongue, I have been tested, I will be tested again
in the modalities of the court minstrels,
the sackbut and the shawm,
down at the corner the unemployed still await their hire,
I raise a curtain from the established confluence
of *right* and *duty*, that mythic patter,
I did not realize you were late for the matinee,
I had planned to share my fears with you,
in 1128 John of Worcester made the earliest known drawing of sunspots,
five days later Korean astronomers recorded the aurora,
I surrender: my architrave, my compass rose,
I am at the mercy of a Baconian simplicity,
tell the child of fire as he arranges and rearranges his toy blocks
I have met the ocean, I have met the mountain,
I have reckoned the isopleth, I come.

BLINK

after Joseph Cornell

This bird's too big for the drawer you've opened,
talons deep in wood like winter sap, feathers ruffed
against the cold that's made a mirror from this puppet day.
In the distance blocks of text move
like heavy animals across the stubble of a field
leashed by their collectivity, by a sign they're seeking within hunger—
artifact of shared concern, tongued as an infant will
for shape, for boundary, admission of territory
as different from portrait as mug shot
is from the fierce eye that tracks each eclipse
and successive enclosure. If a noise like a beating of wings
threatens theft of one dimension, think of the weight
that lifts: half a doubled yolk, procreative
urge ratified by the chill that settles blade-like
at the point where you touch the hollow of my throat
just once. A finger will do. *O World!* A cleaner predation
descending like night blotted halfway now
from black to blue, knowing point of entry
will never be a problem (your quisling
crazed behind you on rough pavement). Immensity
disguised as scale hangs gravity from vision, its milky
pound of flesh, or ounce, twin measures
to reclaim that feral necessity. And so we want to free him, don't we?
—open out into a scripture of small deaths, piercing of flesh,
the needle's cry; think light bulb, splay, think
the darner's skewed instrument, its sly hooked smile.
This tether isn't much, thin strip of hide.
A blind dream burns in my one body. And strains to reach you.
And spread its length along the haunted sky.

VARIETIES OF RELIGIOUS EXPERIENCE

with apologies to William James

I.

I want to lie down in a room of blue sand.

The light is brighter here, or rather
this particular refraction suggests a specific intensity,
mass without weight.
The quality of light is important to me. Apparently. I stumble
from illumination to illumination on sharp miracles.

In the room of blue sand will be a
great moisture, unobtrusive. A cool glistening.

Walking out this morning I enjoy the presence of a companion.
We speak of small things. Around us
the world is busy telegraphing knowledge of surfaces
back to the light which adjusts
on a planetary scale, making due allowance
for velocity and distance. Our bodies take part in this exchange. Blood
rushes to the surface to hear what is said,
relaxes back to appropriate depths.

That I want what I cannot have
is no obstacle, of course. A goad rather.

My companion whistles beside me.
He is an optimist, committed to narrative and therefore
the possibility of redemption. I envy him.

I want to draw a circle large enough in the snow
to hold us both.

II.

Understand: that the room of blue sand presupposes
a house, any kind of habitable dwelling
is a fallacy, though an attractive one.
One imagines crisp linens
and silence punctuated only by a slight
occasional tapping, not unpleasant.

A second misapprehension:
that the mystery of circulation has been explained,
blood and lymph and water.
We know only the architecture of this motion,
a lemma, a kind of shell.
And the faint distant burst of the ram.

Third error: dream of a common language
beyond this spectrum.

For my companion there is no such room, nor should he want it.
Make no mistake, I am not the person
you think, I am entirely
more various than that. And less charitable—

I desire this room for myself alone.
Also, an exhalation of stars.

III.

In my dream, my companion and I stood in a snowy field.
Nothing to mar the new crust, not even
evidence of our arrival.
In my dream my companion and I stood a few feet apart, but together,
at the center of a snowy field.
We stood that way for a long time.

IV.

To posit a mountain is to presuppose
moisture, in this dispensation,
also a certain gravitational flow.
One may add trees, evergreens at the higher elevations.

Phenomenon: subdued thunder of the ram from the spring-hollow,
a clean sound. Though perhaps it is indulgent to say so.

To posit a mountain is,
on the most basic level, to proscribe the idea of translation.
One cannot transcend height.
One can circumnavigate it, but that is not the same thing;
the border of altitude has not been crossed.
This is the difference between a mountain and a river
whose depth though finite implies a singularity.
One can cross a river.
Millions of people do this every day.
For with a river eternity is measured in two dimensions
which is not the same thing at all.

Phenomenon: flow of water from the spring-hollow,
trying to make itself into a mountain.

V.

The faint tapping in the room of blue sand promises security,
which is really the illusion of rest. Not unpleasant.
One counts each audible contact
then measures the silence.

That I wish to lie down at all is at best a grave impropriety.

Also a moist dripping from the walls,
beneath the level of my hearing.

VI.

My companion and I walk down to the lower of the ponds
formed by the stream fed by the spring.
Ice spools within the plane of its expression.
By the race, a clutch of mallards.
The constricted flow creates friction which creates heat
so that a bed of algae opens, even in winter.

Phenomenon: stab of pale beaks in the cold water.

Seven today, four males, three females.
Yesterday there were six.
I cannot help myself—before I know it
I have assigned them a number.

We walk across a low causeway.
My companion is whistling again. He goes a little ahead of me,
his glance moving from side to side
drinking it all in,
the ducks, the ice, the pond,
snow in the branches of the hemlocks and white pines.
He throws back his head and laughs.
From here the ram is inaudible, to my ear at least.
Up a steep hill. My breath comes hard,
visible in the noon sun. I feel the blush of cold-sting in my cheeks
(we know only the architecture of this motion).

I consider the possibility that the room of blue sand may be subterranean.
I consider the possibility it may not exist at all—

I cannot help myself. Before I know it
there is something like delight.

SACCADE

Involuntary movement, enough to keep thin muscles supple: we should be thankful. It's unnerving, though, to watch that lidded spasm in another, sudden jerk and flutter as if the film of self, projector-bound, had torn; and as with damaged film all sounds gone strange, tick of the travel clock a false sequencing, radiator hiss. We never question the heart's pulse or the diaphragm's periodic ascension, its rise and fall like a diving bell, heavy, nineteenth-century. Waking at night I feel my breath hitch, pressure against sternum the doctor says is apnea, the body experimenting with its own death. The sheet that covers us is clean and sheer and I lie almost still beneath it, thick motion of my chest restored. Outside wind hustles boxcars of cold air through the trackyard of white pines. Your fingers brush my thigh then splay against the mattress. Your cords tighten; I catch a fricative and low moan. I think of the lymph circulating in your bare shoulder, pale golden fluid in hidden channels, that thoughtless benevolence. One opens a door to the body and finds a stranger there. Of course. Some nights I feel like I'm drowning, then wake and feel like I'm drowning for one moment longer as the mind, panicked, rushes to double-check its instruments. If I were to reach now I could rest the fingers of my left hand on your eyelids, skin stretched like silk on a roiled surface. It's a kind of blindness, this night-dark, though my eyes are open. What I want is for someone to thrust me beneath the flow of you and stencil a first word.

TROPIC OF CANCER

What one finds threatening another finds organic,
even comfortable, two bars in 4/4 time taped
against a bedroom window; transparent in the same way
the skin is, light penetrating to a certain depth then stopping,
suddenly, as at a root definition. A primary color:
red, yellow. What vacancy will unite this sequence?
Outside stars scrape against the night's file with a precision
we've mapped onto the surface of memory,
Once there was a forest, and we were in it.
Once a man with a sword held a woman's head.
There must have been a tune to go with that, a rhythmic cry.
Still the alphabet evinces a tranquility,
all human endeavor abstracted into a finite
number of strokes, the kind of game a child invents
in a moment of boredom, ad hoc. And teaches to friends
his own age. By bedtime he'll have forgotten the rules . . .
Tell me a story. But the names sleep gives us
have all died from the tongue, syllables caught
between tooth and lip at the moment of waking.
At some point the music assumes an orthogonal suspension,
one player on each floor in a space projected ever upwards.
Does this affect the tuning? Does the Doppler
draw the vertical? And when, precisely,
does the performance end? —Reluctant aseity
twice repeated, first the hard consonant, then the soft.
The spirit of God moved upon those waters.
One wants to believe, yes. One wants in fact
to think of vowels so holy their notation is unnecessary,
a common faith, something to scroll in sand
and ashes while the mind blanks and the hand
moves lightly across a brushed surface. You reach out,
touch the media, feel that faint thrum.

I sing of arms and a man. We begin to remember!
Those that go down to the sea in ships . . .
But the musicians, tired, have long since descended and dispersed.
A single note is heard. As if from a great distance.
I steady the prow of your bones, make you feel normal.
There's a splinter of glass in your pale eye.

HEAVE-HO:

if I could lift the cold from the dress form of this present *yes*
then there's a wildness we wouldn't be missing, a single revelation
spun out into series like kitchen furniture. What originates as abstraction
evolves into fluorescent pulse; in this way the transcendent
becomes useful, that is, acquires an ethical component
unlike the animals in their dull idyll.
Granted some concepts are difficult to grasp. What I can't make out
is the monogram your arrival etches in the sink's dry teething.
—But if the articulation of consent is plural?
Then we dance to supravariant tunes, self-portrait of the poet
as Deaf Man Waltzing: a terrible pun but a more elegant prospect,
not to mention less wasteful of electricity.
So let's talk blame. Last week in Ellettsville, Indiana,
I misread GUITAR LESBIANS for GUITAR LESSONS on a streetside sign.
They're out there, strumming away. My own risk in love
is that some continents will rise or fall before you say your first word.
We could all wear silk armbands to show who's chosen silence.
We could stand very near water and pretend to be bridges,
then others would spraypaint news of their own affections on our thighs
in bright colors. You think I'm joking. But in my dreams
someone is always cutting the bolts from my back.
Try imagining the theoretical as a succession of indigenous archetypes:
predestination, evolution, relativity :: ram, salamander, jackal.
This is the phylum of subjectivity, the genus of cohesion.
After the twenty-fourth dimension our own alphabet's exhausted;
beyond that—pictographs, ideograms, every horseshoe crab that scuttles
could be a proposition by Augustine or the unquiet shade
of that blender we junked last fall. Seriously,
I *demand* a ghost for each machine, I proclaim the acceptable year
of the small power tool. Where's Arthur Murray when I need him?
Wait, it's still a bright spring morning here in Pangaea.

We'll trip the heavy fantastic—watch out for my buttress,
    don't scuff the linoleum.
You say: *He believed large fictions about himself and extended them onto paper.*
I say: *Infidelity*—for now, buzz of an unseen fly.

A DOOR IN THE HIVE

Shaft of light between thunderheads
but no angel yet. Meanwhile one becomes adept.
The code of Third Street, of Jackson Avenue
waxes comfortably familiar.
One begins to live broadly in this air.
One begins to ask questions, for instance
Should I teach the child a new trick.
(—Should *I* teach *this* child.)
Bright June afternoon, lazy
buzz in the myrtle, the lawn a green stutter;
how far we have come—no butterflies
dead in jars, no chloroform,
no thrush or brush of pixellated scales
like graphite against flesh.
Let's say the child is my son.
Around us the myrtles lord themselves into light
like past generations (here, a pressed
Doxocopa pavon in the fretwork
of a mirror, late nineteenth-century).
I teach my son how to tie the string,
gently but snug. Apian shiver.
We have ten seconds, fifteen maybe.
His laughter a high sound, like a nest, the body
beginning to come home to itself.
And take flight, inscribing a raised circle.
Of course: as though to add more color to the picture,
that brilliant blue. My son's voice
bound by the action of the thread he holds,
insensate—the thread I mean
though it carries a faint vibration
down to the surface of each pale fingertip.

Sun behind clouds now, foredraft
a wider circle, luscious
(—*do I teach him how to take it back*)
like bruised fruit. My son's hair
recast from straw-gold to dull flax in a moment.
He asks, *What do we do when we're done?*

JACK DESCENDING

We drop from mid-sky on a slow rope,
hand over hand. *Don't look down* you said
so of course I did, now I've got London in my palm,
with my left foot I can pretend Brussels
is just your bad dream, interface
of altitude with apnea. I check your pulse,
we're still descending. In your throat you carry
a small tune like a brown mouse
you don't want broken. Now the Channel
accepts its first girth, pale orchid between the two knees
of this dangling conversation. I had not wanted
to think about beauty, I was aiming
for a fireproof tax shelter with a B.A. in cell biology
when you called up from the scullery
Size doesn't matter, not true of course
but a touching fiction. So I took your hand
and together we twinned the measure of our interval.
It was your strength mainly.
Before the blade, before narrative
could cast us like seedcorn into atmosphere,
a Socratic argument for the infinitude of memory
which is to say, a retroductive device.
The boy angels ply their trade by day, the girl angels by night
and with each excavation a benign intelligence
winks down. In the meantime
we assign each glance
a pitch, a number, a botanical familiar.
Though we plummet. Though I acknowledge
my base nativity. If these strings survive impact
I will compose a psalm of mourning.
I will demand a detour in the ley lines of Devon,

I will draw the womb tighter
like a sling to its shot, not so much volition
as splendor, your ample form: had I owned that Oedipal thirst,
had I known how your vagary governs the empyrean
I would have kept both feet on the ground.

HORNPIPE FOR SAINTS

From the pink lythrum a double buzz,
one from the bees in their engrossed collectivity
and the other its twin, or image in my brain
pressing out from that center; sympathetic,
desiring that nectar, and in an identical way
devoid of nuance or volition. The acquired taste
is salty, then bitter, and the cry is
simplify, simplify though with each dispossession
words crowd more thickly to their source.
Another difference: we are not
bounded in our passions, acts of aggression
not lethally finite—the greater likeness
therefore is the wasp, that other maker
who stings and stings again even as he plies
his own crisp watermark, indwelling
yet aloft, as we are not, excepting
those clumsy mechanical improvisations
or else the night's dreaming, that purest ambition,
We have cheated death again. Then spasm,
the body's strict account laid open
to gravity's garnish, roused at last into the same light.
Sour ghost of sweetness on the tongue.

PHARISEE'S LAMENT

I am haphazard in my ministrations
but take some comfort in order.
The burden rests on others: the gas man,
the postman, those other faithful
in their convocations, all flesh
moving foursquare across this lively grid.
Even the horses—creatures of habit—
profess their devotion to gods
of oat-box and grass-pasture, twice daily
east and west before the crude stations
of their desire. A ritual, this sacrament of appetite
renewed each morning as the mind
works its soft way from darkness
to the satisfactions of eye, of lip,
a pleasure. The light frays, the horses rise
from the lower field; they know
they will be compensated yet in this dispensation
though their faith is rooted
in the doubtful sinews of an angry man.
I stand in the shadow of the mow
and listen as their bodies touch
and touch again, proximate, expectant.
The stars spin from their dark autoclave.
I draw a long breath, hold it. The mare nickers.
This is one way of loving the world.

IN THE GATE OF SAMARIA

2 Kings 6–7

A pretty verse, *If the Lord would make windows in heaven.* And like
    a collage, red paint spilling

Past the notes. Paste on paper. And the hunger. Two measures of
    wheat for a penny, two measures of barley a penny . . .

But that comes later. *See ye how this son of a murderer hath sent to take*
    away mine head. No patent medicine, no engraved roses.
    Nothing tender this time. *Then he said,*

God do so and more also to me. The old story, yes, but a corollary
    version, faith as forensic archaeology. *Out of the barnfloor, out*
    of the winepress

The universe goes on expanding, signalling uselessly back to us.
    Sankey & Bliss write songs that make the whole world sing

In major keys, barely a hitch to suggest pathos: sympathetic synco-
    pation, not too jazzy. *So we boiled my son*

And I did eat him. But later, with crowds in Chicago, Boston, New
    York. The pews filled with women sighing. So handsome!
    And it came to pass,

When the king heard the words of the woman, that he rent his clothes. This
    is how loss works, "blue," say, rendered into cobalt or
    cornflower, "red" into carmine or scarlet or vermilion. A
    reduction of focus,

A narrowing of aperture: I spy. A sharpening of knives. *And the*
    king said unto her, What aileth thee?

I believe, yes. But this is the rub, denial of the changeling, my first
　　order to wedge the jamb shut. *Is not the sound of his master's*
　　feet behind him? Sweet seraphs those footfalls,

"Tread Softly" sung in honeyed tones, affectuoso. *This woman said*
　　unto me, Give thy son, that we may eat him today, and we will eat
　　my son tomorrow.

Simple, forthright declaratives: "This woman said." "We will eat."
　　"Give thy son . . ." Note the invisibility of the indirect object,
　　i.e., who keeps the counters at day's end

In a nation with a single door. *My father, shall I smite them? shall I*
　　smite them? Repetition for emphasis,

Tread softly, the master is here—dulcet tones, a soulful glance
　　to the mourner's bench. What he wants, Sankey tells *Harper's*
　　Bazaar, is to besiege their better selves. The ladies swoon,
　　they know they should be touched

And so they are, on cue. Floral border to the lithograph print. An
　　ass's head for forty pieces of silver. Dove's dung for five.
　　Admitting, then, the possibility that a wound is necessary

(—A dry season. The elm leaves settling in bright drifts against the
　　dust. Call this *now*—)

In Samaria. *Why should I wait any longer* to execute obsession as a
　　series of ellipses. To mug the shadow cast by the human
　　heart, to use aniline dye,

To draw a map with charcoal on stone. Granted, geography's insufficiency. Presumed, "nation" as "house," a foursquare protocol

Though not many would be raised here. Such oratory, such metaphor, such radiance, such music . . .

So we boiled my son, and did eat him: and I said unto her on the next day, Give thy son, that we may eat him:

And she hath hid her son.

NINE WEST CLAY

Picture a door locked invisibly beyond its one stoop's
dressed stone, a kind of drug you'd take once and then pass on
to friends. Upstairs construction, transistor blare, I was telling you
about time in terms of Minkowski space and event horizon—
Does anybody really know what time it is or can anyone really hear
with all those saxes buzzing, infinitesimal delay
in the radio waves coming in low and clear like a jet
that's ripe for landing. There's a mathematical moment
when it's possible to know
exactly what's happened, the shape my finger traces
on the skin of your inner arm, or a phrase, *This is how ties break.*
This is how home cries, a child's drawing,
red loaf of 'each brick—no vinyl siding, no asbestos—
residence abstracted from environment like a bird from some polled elm
then reduced to typography in two dimensions,
a necessary adjustment, the kind of treaty you sign
knowing you'll break it, later.
Today's program is brought to you by the letter Q and the number 3.
Or, *This is how hope chimes. This is how poems lie—*
plot dependent on will and cell biology
as if spirits could be raised from the dead, boxed into a past
of studs and rafters, dry-walled, tricked out in furnishings
someone's bound to find gaudy, *so Seventies!* "Take a seat"
intoned with literal flourish, not the kind of theft
anyone's likely to report. Out in the street
a siren suggests it's time to get this particular show
on a particular road, fall down blind and then rise up
when a friend strokes your forehead, flushed and damp.
Sometimes it's worth imagining something bigger's out there
if only to feel gravity's specific pull. Call it prayer. Call it trademark,
colophon, station identification projected into eternity,
all those Nielsen households spinning out
one by one into an ether that's more real

with each passing day. So trust me. It's what you've got coming,
you and all those other toll-evaders of the dreamworld
ratcheting around the far bends of the literal, those brilliant corners.
Time out, time was, time's up; time now (yes, time)
for a simpler tune, the space you're growing into, emblem of a disaster
worse than physics, worse than Top 40 even,
history catching up with the body. What Plato should have said
fireside, safe from fallout, wiping ocher from his long fingers:
Brighten the cavern where you are.

CONFESSIONS OF THE MOUSE KING

Rock without scissors yields the same as with.
This paper, for instance: so believe that stone extruded
makes its one pass as this thin ink. Our lady of lithography,
each sewn signature, the cutting and the paste
applied in hopes of some organic connection,
as thigh to hip. In the meantime I pledge my small furnace.
Water is the triumph of necessity over will—
erodes rock, rusts scissors, swells paper back to pulp.
So it's current that sifts estrangement from terror,
same as the night-pull of childhood,
that breathless waking in the dormitory of pressed-back
thefts and exculpations. And all before the advent of doubt,
say, that both hands could render slab or blade
in the same moment. My own crown transmutes the prehistoric.
The skins I'm dressed in are my own.
I keep trying to express myself on a cave wall
but get interrupted by anachronisms, just now a mug of hot coffee
at my left elbow. This is one way of coming into the world.
And one way of leaving it. On the count of three
I find I've become my own rigid constellation.
I heft my rock, tuck my shears into my belt
and use the pages of my manuscript as rungs on an infinite ladder.
Even I can't see them from sideways on.
There's a confusion in the division of labor, suddenly
the air is full of burly angels with their union buttons and shock batons.
I scramble down in haste: no sense in provoking God
by naming Him. Or by conducting a census.
The thing is, every child's a walking reliquary—
shake one and see the blood flow before your very eyes.
In the meantime I have enormous dependencies.
Cut me and I bleed. Poison me and I die.
The only difference between me and Narcissus is that I'm still running,

---

ninety percent of me anyway. The rest is salt and malice.
I keep confusing names with numerical sequences
so if I refer to you as *beloved* I'm just being mathematical.
What attracts me to any system is precision,
the extent to which it bolsters my arguments with the dead . . .
By now it's time to graduate to games of strategy from games of chance.
I'm mounting an offensive against you.
I'm using all my weapons: the text, the foundation, and the knife.
There's a boat resting on the far bank, and there's a reason
I'm telling you this, even if all you are to me now is shadow on a
    struck set's painted flat.
I could change. You could still reach me. Please:
if self is a refuge, then say which.

PROCESSIONING

It must seem so clear to you. How, say, one life opens into another

Then stops, a place in air marking that boundary. A breath, which
    expanded or compressed

Can stake out any volume until released by puncture or loose hand.
    On the best days of course the sky

Is what we'd call a brilliant blue, today a pale turquoise lightening
    to milk at the far edge.

If there's a vanishing point in this landscape I can't see it. Not that I
    don't appreciate the value of discretion; I only

Meant that compassion is dependent on knowledge, unlike charity.

Try thinking of self as the less oblique choice—a house a friend may
    show you, giddy with his art, or the way

Even a held note can force a rhythm, mapmaker's error of closure,
    a misplaced sovereignty. You're right,

Voice proceeds directly from physical form. When I open my mouth

Horizon rushes to fill the cavity: I've got birches brushing, hemlocks
    flossing and that pink bungalow

On Hancock Road resting with a bitter twist at the back of my tongue.

What we need is a more equitable levy. Here's the purse, take it, it's
    yours, smell of supper wafting down

From an upper window. I know it's all for my own good. I know,
you'd kiss me now if there were soldiers here to see.

APOCATASTASIS

For the instruments are by their rhymes,
as Kit Smart wrote. Walking out yesterday
the bud's promise seemed a crystalline
hallucination, spring's early flowing stone,
the maimed sycamores climbing in geometry
grey as steel, as smoke, as the sky
that hangs low as stiff washing from the lines.
Pity small life, the stem that pushes
up from this hard surface, the insensate
bravery. If we anthropomorphize the world,
the night reduces to our capacity for hope
and all tender fallacies. Thus purity.
Thus metaphor's gift, the ice that spools
and circles at skin's surface. My love,
there is no winter but the winter of the heart.
Perhaps this cold will pass. Perhaps
that bridge was not a harp at all.

PROPHECY: VISITATION

And a lamb shall come. One will open
his door and find a ewe on the step, one a ram
quiet-faced, motionless except
for that feral breathing, halation of steam
if it be winter, summer envelope of oil-scent;
the wool an off-white in which spectrum flares hidden
as leaven within a lump of dough. For each
the invitation will issue at a different frequency,
some audible, a held note, say,
extending beneath the surface into living tissue,
something that can be felt in the same way dry skin
brushes forehead midwinter at day's end.
For others an attendant waiting
as if the body, left to its own domestic devices,
sensed the soul's tread at the grate, fumble of keys
at the brass knob. And a white stone.
In which day all blood shall seek recompense
calling forth from the body, carolling as children
on a feast day and those harmonies
recapitulated by atmosphere, wash of silver
among high clouds, copper solution for the burnish:
from a great height beheld, thirty
clicks a minute, and prints hung to dry
in a bright space filled with pine boughs sighing.
The earth's crust thick with punctured motion.
One will say to his neighbor
I called to thee and heard only silence.
One will say to her friend
I saw the earth as a furnace, burning:
lawn-dregs, orchard parings, branches from a river oak
felled in the last great storm, dawn-kindled.

And a harbor choked black with boatmen.
Waiting to ferry us. The treading of those waters
a pale eddy here on the evening breeze.

DELIVERANCE

Then I realized I had read too many poems
about pulling the dead from the living:

ragged cry of cow or horse or pig straining
against the inanimate flesh in its gut,

the human urgency, greasy hands
reaching deep into unimaginable places,

groping around, arms stiff against the creature's
useless labor, trying to hold on, trying

to bring out the fetal pieces already half-rotten
in the placenta's wash. Sometimes the animal dies,

sometimes not, and everyone human
goes home thinking about the change in life,

what great mystery approached
in the palm's proximity to alien heartbeat,

what small nation, vigorously defended.
But it's only the dumb rhythm of begetting:

with or without us that poor carcass
would have found the air. The same tall grasses

would grow in the rainy season. Late at night
we would still wake to find ourselves

shivering for no reason, no reason at all,
fresh from that hard dream of safety.

II

THE LONE AMISHMAN
TO THE MISSIONARY WOMAN
Dream Song, West Field

Wire me a warning, elaborate the circuitry
of threat's combustion, charged and channeled, map
the veins of fire that flex within these plaster walls.
No one knows better. From your distance
all risk becomes a motherboard suspended
within probability, between *can* and *do*, a vetted system
denied the introjections of the flesh but dependent
on every word and shifting member,
the arm that rises to stroke or strike, the leg's
loose sack and matching vector
lifting hard into regret, the shock
like blood, like iron on the tongue, and borne as easily
past the small wreckage of each private discontent.
You dwell apart, in open space; that clithral
tether sets your pulse to jumping—you assign slim chance
a random number, and call it God
but this to you is *prudence.*
I build with straw and stone. I build with steel
that rises cold within its frozen fluency,
I bear the curse that keeps me scratching at this dirt
as if to shuck the body's bone-pure need.
And you cajole. And you admonish. Mark this,
I may turn, I may yet feel the surge
that sets my feet into the rhythms of their winter dance.
And I may come to you, like a filing you may be welded
tight beyond the surplice of your first intention,
held fast. Not my doing, though I would have you.
Night threads its dark lemniscate. I'll shine,
I'll catch your oiled shadow as we fall.

[AFTER THE MURDER]

after the murder when men rise into the moon
I will be thinking *larceny*, I will be thinking *spandrel*,
I will be thinking anything except coterminous resolution
of the ineffable, I will express this absence as euchre,
I will cast lots for each trick as it falls
in the signature of this or that affection,
I will not meet their gaze, I will exchange my own
excess for a battered valise or else
a spangled trellis, I will dowse for the source
of that spring, that doxic clarity, I will offer cash,
after the murder my pockets will overflow in the soft light
spackling the inside of my schoolboy globe
illuminating the undersides of nations,
the living and the dead, I will engrave an open border
between feeling and action, between trespass and consequence,
I will accept the citizenship of my exile
as they lead me into a wider circumference,
I will raise my eyes to the roof boss of a productive fidelity,
I will bridge the river of my enclosure,
I will inscribe an island on the wrist of my nearest blood kin
without reference to politics, I will vote, I will adopt
the autarchy of a commendable introspection,
I will place one foot in front of the other,
I will spring the trapdoor of my forced amaryllis,
I will lift each pebble from its clay pot as I wash my own hands
in that icy water, I will accept this gift—your cheek—
though now they take all else from me.

VERTIGO

Shaft-mouth one is aware of that drawing, gut-clench in which presence
    at the lip implies presence at a greater depth, therefore velocity

With its spectral shift, lush green of periwinkle and honeysuckle
    running down to black against red clay, infinitesimal Doppler
    modulation of the bees that descend

In search of one more sucrose extrusion. We see: iron bedstead, ragged
    upholstery of a couch snagged where the first lateral tunnel

Recapitulated this dispensation in terms of earth and ore. Appliance
    skeletons. Not a stable place, one picks one's way

Through briars and scrub elm with care as if a heavy tread could
    dislodge some internal synchronicity, the way it did once at New
    Straitsville, the miners free in that moment

To see their earth on fire; or at Centralia, the surface withdrawing like
    the shoreline of a dead sea, pulling

More tightly in upon itself in smoking temblors. Here the prize was
    copper which melts but does not burn, and for a few years only—

No town, company shacks long ago collapsed into punk-board or else
    carted off for timber. Sun-dapple, drone of the bees as they rise
    and fall

And rise again, programmed toward hidden hives. What we would call
    a quiet place. Sweat-itch at collar and sole:

No one goes there, said the woman at the end of the road, *except they have something they want to get rid of.* Not affective in the same sense; a scandent

Twilight. Lifting sweetness this time from a single string. And the forms more various. Licit we should come so far.

MUCKING OUT

Winter coming, and the stall knee-high
in dung, in places: symptom of a distracted season.
In mid-afternoon heat my horse
is disinclined to leave the barn.
I force him out with the fork
and start the excavation: hard work
but no harder than any other
necessary penance, and not so dirty as some.
I'll sing a happy tune. A bright day—
outside the piebald trees
glint like polished rocks. The light
enters the barn through slats in parallel formation
like a harp's strings, vibrating
in the quick play of illuminated dust.
Just outside my horse paws the red clay,
stalks angrily off; returns,
sniffs the pile growing by the north gate
with indifferent curiosity.
He lives in the Euclidean geometry of the present,
is unaware of the dispensations,
his own shed self. Above us
the October sun rings
like an iron bell. One hour, the hard-packed
and the friable, loose, air-light, drifting
chaff between the tines;
beneath them the ink-muck still glistening.
If distance is God's way of addressing the will
then high up, a jet lays its crabbed hand
against the sky's blank score.

NOLI ME TANGERE

I.

No perfect metonym, no pure distillation.
Every wall I raise
is broached before I set my soldiers at the arrow-slits.
I missed that high school lesson:
letters carved into the bark of an oak, immense,
      untraceable.

                      A child travels further
        and further from self, wild terrain rising in altitude,
               inland brush fading from basin to basin.

The child is immaculate.
She will never grow old, she presses the blank face of a dream
to her tired eyes and thin lips. She is the absence
and repository of all signifiers.

2.

                        Ecce faber, then.
             To invest the soul in imagination,
      in the prescribed economy. This patch of earth.

[Consider:

PITY IS NO MORE THAN DISTANCE WRAPPED IN SENTIMENT,
    COLLUSION WITH THE EXPANDING UNIVERSE.
      or
PITY IS BUT DISTANCE WRAPPED IN SENTIMENT,
    COLLUSION WITH THE UNIVERSE, EVER EXPANDING,
      SIGNALLING USELESSLY BACK TO US.

or

I REJECT PITY, ITS COMPOUND
OF DISTANCE WITH SENTIMENT.

—The argument thusfar]

affixing some stray resonance.

3.

She is the absence and repository
of all signifiers. She is hungry. She walks
or is carried
a long way, through sandy hills.

—Do you want to believe this?

(And what does it mean, then, being a child?)

4.

Do you want to believe she wanted to return.

Do you want to be certain, do you want
to propel that single photon along its journey

to the mirror,

presuming, for the moment, the existence of a lid
we call *time*. Presuming, for the moment, its suspension:
the bracken,
the flat rocks of the falls,
salt tang giving way to bearblossom.
And will *when* matter,
so that I can call it *rape* for you; is that
what you're thinking. Your finger
loose on the trigger.

Do you want her to survive.

Or, do you want to *be* the mirror. Or,

(5.)

do you want to be that certain.

6.

The brush of green blades against her footsoles.

7.

Do you want this to be about race.

—*When I open my heart*
there's an infinite paper cut-out
strung accordion-like, hand in hand, every figure
its own simulacra.

—*When I open my heart*
I think the tree gap in the south line
holds the last coal of available perfection.
I could reach with my left hand, cover that space
where the light gives all
appearance of failing. Babies know this, like poets
reaching for the moon's flat disc.

—*When I open my heart*
two moths flutter from the wound, wet and pulsing.
One light, one dark.

Or, do you want this to be about sacrifice.

8.

The fact of the body, ineludible.

[Meaning: the wheel is false
(the burning spokes) (the revolution).
Or, the hair on which I travelled to this place, that slender
ear of wheat, ripe in its dull cairn.]

9.

The rain came later that night.
I was feeling my way past a yew hedge.
I was feeling my way past a wall of smooth stone.

And then a sudden lowering, as a bird
declines in altitude through a series of calibrated
displacements
toward its goal. Coda of uplift.

At first there was a flatness, and I wanted to join it,
to extend my body through the three points that define a simple plane.

Her figure in powder blue (1937).

The foliate pyrography. A continuous weave—
(call this *purity*—)
Each ray
her triumph, my long home.

LUMINOUS BODIES

That lucidity could draw such associations,
regardless of distance. Sandstone and cinder. And the vectors
of desire converging in empathy, in natural sacrifice.
The infinitive again: to be, to call, to resurrect
meaning volume rendered constant
past the emulsion of recessive views. Likewise the eye's captivity,
its classical debate. Corpuscular. Or not. A constant
intromission to the soul's source as to fire.
Vision, then, devolves to a species of touch:
penetration and pattern. Plato's theory, according to which
a stream of light issues from the observer's eye and coalesces
within the optic field. Like Ezekiel's wheel, like Mary at Lourdes,
both *motions returned to the soul.*
"For particles are continually streaming off
from the surface of bodies, though no diminution
of the bodies be observed, because other particles take their place."
Such vivid economy. If this were about language I'd sing.
If this were a folk poem I'd place a single ant
high in the firmament, awaiting contact.
"As when a man, thinking to go out
through the wintry night, makes ready a light, a flame of blazing fire,
putting round it a lantern to keep away all manner of winds:
it divides the blasts. But the light, the finer substance,
passes through and shines on the threshold
with unyielding beams." So the pupil, so the cornea,
so *the achievement of that state*
in which transparency is no longer potential,
but actual, such that bodies separated from the observer by the medium
become visible. As in cloud, as in granite, as in cedar.
And the medium a continuation of the object,
brought into the eye's small chapel. *Since the mountain will not come*
to the observer, the observer must go to the mountain.

For this is the hunger that binds the starlings in their collective.
For this is the incunabula of the soul's instruction.
For this is the logic of the Beloved, *video te, ergo sum:*
this violation. This is the mote in God's eye.

GOLDBEATER'S SKIN

Ask for an axe, a syringe, a length of rope
plein air, coiled or loose. Working from nature dilates focus,
draws form from its pale circuit—point beyond which
each sphere reckons its ovation.

Ask for a clip, a pin, a charge, a powder.
Denounce the offset: heaven knows the personal
expands to fill a visual field, colonnade or any aural space
incurred as penalty. Ask for self, ask

whether the white you see is application
or absence, content or context, eight ducks rubbed
into glacial moraine, pinfeathers scarlet against slate-grey scree:
one landscape out of many, call it "Off-Season,"

call it "'58 Chevy," ask for a blade, a vial,
a flashcube, a spool of fresh film. It's important
that the work have a handmade quality, not the disconnect
of digitized tablets scaled just short of empathy

or market value. Request a hearing,
query the epic. Notice how images rise to within
a finger's breadth but come no further, pain excised from touch.
This is the refuge between notation and balance.

It shreds in transposition. So ask for a permit,
a thrombus, a roadside stand; hot wax, at least a thimbleful.
Somewhere in these battlements an egg lies hidden.
I promise, when we find it, Naples falls.

CANTICLE
FOR THE SECOND SUNDAY IN LENT

To be the son of a poet is to lust in a great circle. Places both of you will
    visit, for instance—Iowa cornfield, New England farm midwinter.
    A mill-race. Plaque for the bell factory hidden now

By upthrust suspension, spray from which flow freezes even gravity's steady
    ictus, compressing this river into a held note. Somewhere nearby
    a clock ticks

But not loudly. One draws a breath, holds it in the pale hour between
    delight and grief aware of genetic precomposition, the chest's
    scripted rise and fall. The idea that history

Is more than the sum of component parts glosses pain with sentiment,
    yet we do it all the time, sitting together with friends after the
    roof's caved in. Bitter words from the beloved—

A wild complaint, as in the *Donal Og* with its impossibilities and smooth-
    stripped compass rose: *It was a bad time she took for telling me that;*
    it was shutting the door after the house was robbed . . .

There is the lament, and then the assignation; shocks of ice piling up
    in the lee of the dam, and voice plucked knife-edged from a chill
    breeze. In the fable those children and that livestock

Were replaced, not restored, two different things. This evening the sky
    leaves wind-knots tied in your footsteps, bits of string and grass
    blown up from some uncovered place.

No longer a scrawl. In which some letters may not be spoken. You write
    around them as on the rim of a wheel revolving slowly to the rhythm
    of sleet against a kitchen window,

Promising nothing this time: no ships, no towns, no seaside courts.
  Only the tannin-dark water you came from. And the green fields
  in the high passes to which you will go.

Stooping in the dooryard the boy saint picks up the body. He is curious, he begins to massage the tissue around the eyelids; begins to pluck, feather by feather, then the skin—a deeper massage—pulling away from the cranium. It is not his firm pressure that accomplishes anything, he is merely part of a larger process that would take longer were it not for his assistance.

He does not think *sparrow.*

He thinks, vaguely, *bird.* He thinks, more specifically, *skull*: it's the bone he wants, near shimmer, its pallid shoal.

His own hand is a skeleton reaching after a skeleton. This is the first lesson of desire: like to like. The fruit comes later.

Time passes. He thinks it is wrong to laugh at clowns because his grandmother tells him they were born that way, delivered from the hospital with bulbous noses and orange hair. Later he paints clowns, faces copied from financial magazines, glossy inserts, *TV Guide.* He dresses them up in his mind, applies the pancake and mascara, the outrageous prosthetics. He tells himself he chooses these faces because they are strong faces. They are all male.

He paints women too, many women, first as nudes, then flensed, then as skeletons. He paints hominids, he paints apes. He paints hominids painting. He paints painting apes. He paints a male chimpanzee bent over his easel and palette, sketching a female nude.

He does not think of painting a female chimpanzee sketching a male nude.

He paints a woman from the neck up. He paints a woman from the neck down. He paints three women as they pass a peach from hand to hand. He etches a woman cast upright in snow: sex, navel, eyes, breasts.

He becomes a teacher. He argues that all art is figurative; that the figure ceases to matter only when we cease to be human. He is very sure of this. He thinks all art occurs in its own time. He memorizes: fossae and tibia, coccyx and acetabulum, calcaneus and teres.

He paints his wife slipping out of the musculature of her upper back as from an evening gown. He paints himself holding his own skin.

He paints a python, curled around a branch, straining to draw a hunter's shaft from its body with its own bloodied mouth.

WHAT BEGINS BITTERLY
BECOMES ANOTHER LOVE POEM

The earth has a taste for us, in its unknowing
appetite there yet resides a hunger, incompletion
that draws all life to its dark self. What, then,
shall we say of the flesh's own desire, distal
thumb-brush at evening? There is nothing to say,
the vowels cluster uncertain in the beautiful vase
the throat makes, fricatives corralled behind
ridge of gum and bone-splinter. Flesh and earth:
fire is an illusion, to which water is the antidote.
The day was a bright one, there seemed no need
to move about with mirrors, the usual circumspection
and indirect approach. The abundance of small life
argued some measure of clemency, likewise
the Jerseys lowing in the paddock breeze, tender
shoots of cress and sweetpea spiralling upward.
But fire is a cruel hoax: now you see it,
now you don't, the object of your affection
cast in carbon on the hard ground which will,
in time, receive. Roadside the irises bloomed
two or three feet max above soil's surface,
rough tongue resting lightly on each leaf, each
violet exclamation. In full sun your hand guided mine
to the wound. A small one. Water and blood,
like the nurse said: prestidigitation of the body.
We stood without shadows on asphalt at midday.
What we call patience is only fire again, compressed.
I remember: your face flushed, stray petal lodged
in the damp whorl of your dishevelled hair.

III

WHAT GOES UP

two lines from Attila Jozsef

Hell is the stuff of the human mind, witness
how the etiquette of the damned holds
our not inconsiderable attention—
their malice, poisoned gestures, their compassion
(yes, in hell as here) wasted on the self
else abstracted into piety. Tantalus
we know, the ripple and the branch that move
in constant thwart of his intent; Sisyphus
with his stone and inclined plane—
simplest classical solution—our thought on afternoons
like this, heat tight between collar and nape,
posture to anthracite half-ceded.
But machines have their own way, the one
who feeds them is the one they obey, in this case
mass by means of gravity upon which
(again, abstracting from the source) we cast
a god's name, our mean stature magnified.
Imagine, briefly, these lines
in another language, chosen at random
or for sheer euphony: of no commercial use,
Malagasy, Welsh, Hungarian thinning out
like atmosphere to the edge of exile.
There's no harm in improving the days
as they lengthen, you strolling lakeside, early spring,
I handing a pear to my young son.
Speech is an owl that flies from us in daylight
pursued by crows. What we want
is a glass of water, a little quiet. Even a blue sky
bears weight and density. Even Dante's pen
stumbled, at the gates of paradise.

QUALIA

First subject: the division.
For some vision for some division.
For some and for others, for the verb *could*.
As in get, as in have, as in be.
For some the fruits of a pleasant employment.
For some a long sleep. And the division
adequate for others in pursuit
without which a blank seeming.
And for the some the gilt
verb chugging now orthogonal now parallel
like the others in their swift passage.
Away from the some.
Away from the *is,* the charmed
indicative. Duly noting the night invoked like dark fire
to cover the some in their sleeping
the other in his waking
her midnight pain. And touched by a spark
the verb lifts. A physical fact, a distinct isonomy
as in bring, as in set, as in cry
speaking the tongue of division
a gambit a small unhanding. And others
crowded thick in among the some
in their long sleep. Second subject: that same motion.
Hooked like windows into the light of the others
their days their waking days.

WEDGE

What I wanted first and foremost was distance; I had no understanding.
    Say, that a leap implies an anchorage. A place in space. A
    vector,

A parabolic arc. I chose mathematics. This was better than the old
    drama, so much soap and water. I chose a city

Not unpleasant in the spring, broad streets laced like muscles in the
    palm, Bradford pears flowering. Sometimes

It was like that, the present in my grasp. I could lift it to my lips
    and tongue its shape, the way infants do, all those polished
    surfaces

To which I applied myself without reserve. Forward thrust. Matrices
    of possibility. Trained in knot theory I kept two lengths of
    twine in my desk drawer

Just in case, presumption of a pattern in two dimensions. I walked
    through parks at midnight without once scenting my danger

Which made me vertical, a kind of public monument, my movements
    an inscribed web; what you wanted

Though no more charitable for the imbrication. Some found me a
    kind man. They were mistaken, really

Compassion is just one more posture from which to view the actual,
    impulses in strict procession though less harmful to the scenery.
    Inductive. Then an end to numbers

Except for the heaven in which Stein counts. I believe in that. Vast array of cities not unpleasant in spring, substrate logic of each commercial dream—

There is also history, that other separation.

VALENTINE FOR MYSELF AT THIRTY-ONE

Time passes. My body learns to be content with itself.

The bed in which I sleep now is the same one,
carved by my grandfather before my birth, in which I've slept
since I left the crib—a bit short for my present frame.
I sleep at a slight angle, northeast to southwest.
I sleep on my side, pillow crooked in one arm, usually the left.
From the evidence it appears I toss and turn.
I dream, sometimes terribly: I am a man

who remembers dreams. In this I perceive no blessing.

Late at night I lie on my back in darkness,
listening for the whippoorwills or for my horse
going past the south window on his way to the upper pasture.

There are seven in my generation, none married now
though all have known love's measure. Four such beds among us.
The ache within is not entirely answerable,
flesh to flesh. The mind paces in its bone cage.
I am a man of narrow vision, in a small house at evening—

Time passes. I rub the soreness from my feet—

I resolve to plant a cutting of wisteria, a patch of mint
or some other herb in the dooryard clay.

SANCTUARY

Too much life to go on burning: crows with their outsized tracks,
    deer whose twilight prints freeze into near-rock, quick blaze of
    fox at field's edge. No cause for pillage; one relaxes

Into thoughts of a safe place. White pine and birch abet the illusion
    whispering to themselves in a March breeze as they always have,

During King Philip's War, for instance, amid epidemics, or when this
    town, river-clenched, kindled

In the flood of 1938. The Corps of Engineers dammed the falls,
    made a bit of park at the site: picnic shelters, iron benches
    lakeside not much used. Back in town a willow

Gives rise to a conceptual unity *and* a social division. We can't even
    agree on the site of the old mill: I say just north of the library,
    you're sure it stood east of the brook, with a catwalk and pillars

That could have been saved, long after the building went. A
    musician's cottage burns. He loses everything, notes sublimating
    not into music but into sparks that fill the night sky

For a little while. No one tells his story beyond this moment.
    Downtown there's a new gym we can't use yet

And yes, the snow at the pinnacle of the plow-drift outside my door
    looks just like that Currier & Ives print of a city on fire. You may
    have seen it:

In the left foreground troops and civilians stream across the river on
    a wooden bridge, stray boards floating in the abutment eddy—a
    realistic touch,

Somehow we are glad for the artistry now with the first thaw upon
us and the sky stretched sheer like blue fabric. Not denying the
passion: grateful rather, today's last sun

Bright on the meadow. The ministry of the hand a long one though
we are glad for that call. The pines sniff vaguely, half-remembering.
The candles of winter gutter in their cold flame.

ELBERTA

You should be so lucky as to make that journey.
Orchards planted when I was a child
are already abandoned else uprooted, too old
to bear the market's weight. Outside Inman,
east of Greer packing sheds lean into the future
the same way trees do, gnarled, low to the ground
as if gravity were a defense for children,
a child's game really, requisite
sing-song adumbration. Stein was right, heaven
is the place where we finally have the leisure
to speak the truth to objects
in proper sequence, functions of the body
or of the mind irredentive to that order.
The signs read PEACHES. The signs read
FIREWORKS, CIGARETTES, LAST CHANCE!
either side of the four-lane piled high
with pruned branches, whole trees bare now
in the March sun, good for nothing but burning.
Heading north the exits tick backward
from the singularity of the border, a wide space,
another sign. Faint blur of blue smoke:
it's the sweetness we can't do without,
that sets us planting again, seedlings wrapped
in white tape against late frost. Come June
we'll buy a bushel from some roadside stand
off Route 11 where we used to drive when we wanted
to feel the world suspended for our benefit.
The past answers itself in its own range—
dogs hear it, same as they do those tin whistles.
They understand love, tails wagging at our feet
while we let the juice run down
our chins in some sandy lot. Never minding

that it stains. Never minding that the dogs
aren't ours, just some farmer's curs kept around
to keep the coons at bay. We'll drive on,
night will fall and those dogs will howl at the moon
same as if it had a number. They're lonely for us
though all we are by now to them is a smell.
Around us branches whisper in the June dark.
We're the fire they didn't see coming.
Relent: from the Latin, *re* plus *lentare*,
to bend again. Now turn left. Here, trust me.
Your touch will let us know where we are.

VENDIBLE AESTHETIC

Science says: if you sit with your back to a wall you create a space

Open wing-like, a hyperbola in three dimensions projected obliquely
   into a fourth

By valence of choice. The wall may be inscribed with a gentle
   cream latex, faux panelling or else

Fixed by application of a misguided unity. That figures move

When we fail to face them, just beyond the periphery of vision is a
   pandemic conceit though no less true

For gravity's pull, subtle warp of brick and canvas, cold flow

Beyond the heart's propulsive syncopation. Meanwhile the angle
   a door makes admits a fresh contingency,

Translucence compromised. The chair itself a gesture toward flesh's
   end. From this vantage

The possibilities are indeed endless, both to the right and to the left;
   what Lear called *world* is prepared to make

Any lateral adjustment you may require so long as you do not turn,
   do not

Reach past the frame of that other surface. First the equation, then
   each derivative paring backward from that core—

A wild eloquence. Faint taste of salt on love's split tongue.

THE TREE AND THE CHILD

She said *The twigs had a sort of evil quality, for me.*
She was thinking bodies, whalebones, Victorian collars
flattened to monotype, fabric
bought at yard sales, or inherited.
And that gradual ebb, the one note dying out
of the personal, diminishing until it became a felt thing,
or barely felt, as ions in advance of weather
prick maimed flesh. The rain came later that night,
petulant somehow, like Bosch overpainting a donor's face
and like Bosch also with his small army. She thought
In this vision the owl will have blue eyes.
She sat up in her bed and waited, *his gaze directed at me,*
will he draw me away, seeking what quarry?
Thin band of phosphorus flicking past; that much,
at least, was new, not like the silver ray
tracing its delicate filigree, its bucket
up from the well of deep feeling, the moss a waxing sheen
but slow, easily displaced by hand or other friction.
How did the psalm go? *Let all work*
define a hollow axis, inside a pulse like a spine
and the spine entered, tapped, so sweet
even thirst receded, at least as far as the nightstand.
She has forgotten the equation.
Death is the child she chose not to have,
a curious boy on his low stone wall, legs dangling,
kicking idly, *What's this life of yours? What's love? Why*—
His foot dislodges a stone from its mortar.
She stoops to pick it up, teaches him the old drunkard's game:
nine points, three lines to etch a synthesis.
Soon he's absorbed. She walks on,
presses the blank tablet of a dream
to her lips and tired eyes. *But I remember the flood,* she thinks,

I remember the ocher of the evening train. It's not the same story, it's the only story. Now the hubris and the siege.
Now teeth shielding lips from tongue.

ERRANTRY

I agree, no sense in searching
beneath the oaks. Their stiff towers. Nor the prefecture
of the thorn. In which all moments conspiring
toward their particular ends
as from a long distance. Discalced.
But not without one remarkable garment
which I unfasten which I fold back
like the lid of a heavy chest.
And leave here, neatly gathered. Expecting no recompense,
no parley with the vertical. My sober defense.
Still a blister rises. Miming a martyr's course, precise
spot where the forehead, uncomprehending,
embraces its parent conceit
bringing forth the usual sweet spring
refracted into parable,
then architecture. I ask you. Your name
can't be the word I'm looking for.
But if I were to walk in my sleep under the canopy
I'd sue only for a cool drink
from your pitcher from the extension of your right hand.
Oblique to the thigh's inscription, its bloody wrangle.
Now at evening I pull the door tight
against the wanderer. Not the balm you imagine.
Its hour has yet to come.

PASSION: PATERNITY TEST

Much weariness in watching.
The days move one by one through pine air
like the bodies of men, footsore, neither seeking
nor expecting consolation. In this country
the roads go everywhere, everywhere
and so *asphalt* replaced *macadam*
because the latter, in reference to the individual
will and supervention, proved too personal,
not to mention evocative of such outdated concepts
as Genesis and original sin, complicity
binding like tar—quaint Scottish *mac*
though contracted, though elided now
as is our presence in the landscape, linguistic remnant
wasted beneath a roadcrew's applied devotion.
Complicit, yes. In that we ignored the flags,
the banners and the pennants and assorted
nylon aspidistra with their mottos and detersive emblems,
believing, we thought, in the thing itself,
neither the sign nor the signified
but that sliver which could be documented—
not impartially, perhaps, but with some measure
of communicable reassurance. For example,
the Bremen exit on I-20. For example,
There is cruelty and then there is delight.
West Georgia highway at moonset, mica in the asphalt
like stars that would not otherwise
reflect brute export. Trucks streak by
in rumor of their own passage, which seems right.
Change in the seasons. As if we could. I can't see you
but suddenly I'm not hungry anymore.

THE HEAD OF THE CORNER

Of course I reach for you,
I have never questioned the script
though bundled inside it's invisible, never obvious,
it's the shadow that walks further and further
from the poem on a dark afternoon,
this is the signature year
of the owl, the prodigy's abandoned valise,
there's no sense in wanting
but we do, incessantly, we fall
like iron filings from a lathe's lap
of muddled stars, after which
no corrective exposure, no arctic glare,
seducer and seduced—alike—
I did not say *shiver,*
fate appoints her trim denial, else appeal,
Will you won't you will you won't you will you
won't you join the dance,
that I displace at all
should mean nothing, otherwise
a world stiffens—vanishes—
this is the way with worlds,
multiplication, complicity, and decline,
I am a permanent resident, I am warm-blooded
after the manner of my kind,
do you not yet understand
the comparison, I walked out today
in a pinprick mist at low tide,
I paced above the cold stink of the flats
and presumed that the most obvious motion
must be the most valid,
I want so desperately to believe
that something is missing,
do you not yourself look up at night

and suspect as much,
from time to time,
shall we not then relieve the gambler
of his burden of contempt, her wet wool shawl,
I am reading now from the act and scene
in which you angrily declaim,
I am dressing stone for the bridge we are building
though I know it requires a body,
this is an ancient custom,
I could do it with my eyes shut,
what cause have you for the accusation
or what order do you defend,
do you remember when a bowl of fruit was sufficient,
the chiseled crystal, the ripening flank,
I still long for the aurora,
have I defied Chekhov's dictum, choose then
your weapon, your Trojan demesne,
I will bear it before you,
I have tired of the magic lantern,
can't we just go out for a quiet meal,
Italian perhaps, I am brave enough for that much,
must I capitulate, must you carry
the child I surrendered to the boatman
in your pale arms?

PALINODE: COTTON MATHER

Praying always. But in the literal sense?
In the bath? Under the dull breath
of any given second, like his particular faiths?
—Exemplary mutterer, moving through days
with his great mind always fluttering
in the dark cave of his mouth, his manic concern.
He meant well, we might say, and late in life
gave up the constant patter, the need
to bring the world into being, moment by moment,
himself. *Watching thereunto with all perseverance*
and supplication for all saints. Fair enough:
he persevered, maintained the mission of his public id,
and his supplications, if unheeded, were at least
archived in the libraries of New England.
When I lived in Boston I liked to walk
down past the Common to where the cherries bloomed
in their plots of grass and scored slate,
product of a more decorous generation
though perhaps less prescient: all that careful
horticulture, prayers of hope and terror trembling
on the lips of the women as they left the tomb.
They mistook Christ for the gardener.
As for Mather, his ashes have long been reabsorbed
into the city he helped fix upon said hill.
What he would have wanted? Probably not:
a hard man, though supple in his genuflection
to the order nature brings; this would have been
his Sodom. Now with spring in the air
I lean once more against the oak bench and bargain
what's left of my own heart for mercy on the tongue,
that darkling zeal, those exclamations.

CIRCUS MAXIMUS

I plead no special service.
Night comes, night stretches forth its ambition
like a white hand, like a soldier
new in his pressed blues. And like the night
I bear my weapon. I walk from house to paddock,
I skirl the milk-surface of the trough
and I presume. This benison. Or another,
swift commingling of the spectrum
in the vegetable eye, the sun's
twilight prognostications. With which the ebbing of empathy.
Or: the invocation of a more illustrious origin,
language appropriate to the encounter
between glass and the intromission
of intelligence, disparate.
But I am the heir of the hawthorn.
I am the sillion, the fugitive holograph,
the alkaline seed. I will break the clod that made me.
I will sleep with the silenced stars.

SYNDERESIS

Outside snow traces the same faint absence, same
production ethic, motion extracted from economies of scale
without benefit of clergy. This is a cold music but music nevertheless.
The difference between D-sharp and E-flat lies in the composition
of the chord: in this case trees, light, water. In fact
I cherish the idea of a world beneath this one with a breath of its own.
Two points in space define a line which stretches forth
indefinitely, words gathered like keys on a ring
independent of longing. We won't think of them until one's lost.
Jacob saw angels ascending and descending, the color of salt
in moonlight. Perhaps the color of snow. It's easy
to confuse the igneous with the metamorphic, to give in
to the ground's didactic lost-boy cry. Call it sleep.
Call it halation of hydrogen and oxygen encrusting the soul
at cave's mouth like an electrical charge. In dreams my fingers
wander over your closed lips, a kind of Braille.
I raise one hand in darkness and see all five of my motives—
such spectacle! Such tender hardness of heart.
The note that comes to my throat is D-sharp, the one above middle C:
it doesn't harmonize with your body or with the breeze
eddying in protest at the windshield's glass,
rather with the green the trees were making, then, busy
in that last hour of sunlight after heavy rain.
I'm not torn, exactly—there's a language in me
feeling its way out from a constructed center.
And the muscles of the throat always working, working . . .
The body bears no memory of pain. In the mind, only a projection.
In the flesh a map, like all maps divining a specific gravity.
We keep paying for another chance to wrestle it down,
another lift back to the summit. When is holiness an abridgement of
    taste?
Or what's another exhortation to posture, more or less,

one more classical allusion? Call it elegance,
concinnity, a period style; the wages I'll pay this guard at shift's end.
Though I would not deny the passion, by any means.
All around us now matter is succumbing to night's chill instrument.
I'll follow if you won't look. In this month of the first frost
your face is still my breath on glass at morning.

ANIMAL MAGNETISM

Without a physiological explanation
the question begged by the text is immaculate,
an actionable offense. No doubt this seems familiar—
public—a kind of billboard exercise.
Such as, a man down on four legs.
Such as, a dog up on two
defining a span, a certain lapse of time
in which humanity may be imputed,
falsely as it turns out and for meretricious purposes.
Hence the phrase *You dog*
and its cognates, *yellow, cowardly. Low-down.* It's true,
some people move at high speeds toward dizzying heights
and back again just for the thrill of it.
This clarifies the odds in the short run,
measures the distance between patience and faith.
Watch now, a quick shell game:
when you (the mark) make your choice
God's hands are empty.
Still He washes them.
Floating in the basin, that same dirt
with spittle could cure the blind. But does not.
And you (the mark) poorer for your gamble
moving on, your weight guessed,
your height recorded,
your companion licking tears from his master's eye.
Six letters bind the hollow of your forearm
in one recursive motion
somewhere between *glyph* and *rune*
but without consequence, the way a beggar practices his case
scatting the details of his own tribulation.
It's the Janus face, like playing a rape scene for laughs.
And you are not to blame,

sauntering down now past the booths
and barkers who read you like the open book
you've taught yourself to be. Behind you,
a voice distended into a thin cry. Almost a howl.
In your pocket spare words yet clinking.

PREEN

Be not ungenerous with the mind's Zeus, its cake of salt
and net threaded against delay's languor, emplumed,
paddle-footed skirling the surface of the lake
the body makes. There's grace in this habitat, a buoyancy
bound less by media than intent, indiscriminate hunger
so pure the crusts it's thrown yet go down dry.
Even violence has a purpose here, the latch and then the hybrid,
exemplary reproach—resplendent—an entity
so near to us we clear the space between dress and thigh,
between knife and throat, French-curved path back to first connection
without reference to paternal bond. Written in blood,
in the language of recursion and mineral surprise: RSVP
this casual sacrifice, replete with text drawn down
from myth to asphalt, the feast in full swing—heedless—
paper napkins trampled underfoot, each inscribed
with its cocktail legend. Decorous. Or slipped
into pockets and purses as keepsakes, the kind of cynosure
the god himself resented and rejected, cathexis evident
and suitable for framing. We can't resist its lure—
the aesthetic concentration—three steps closer and the pattern
resolves into lace of brushwork, each lexical ridge
casting finical shadow, small and precise.
In such moments it's consequence we curse, not choice
while on the bank our wish at its most ungainly
hobbles toward a night's rest no less sweet for all its piercing hiss
and zealous hygiene. Pledged to fidelity we lower the blade,
fan out into brake and tangle for what we hope
has caught there, crepitant, rustling. No longer giving thought to flight,
pulse rather; abdicating no high office, no pedigree.
For we are honorable men. Appealing to our advocate.
Wanting only to make the real more real.

COLUMBUS CIRCLE

Off-ramp there's a modulation from *there* to *here*,
a kind of green sign gone flickering, and not from choice.
Now we're circling in the neighborhood
of monuments, we glimpse one and then another through the
    windshield,
proximate, but just so. No one's around
except for construction workers bottoming out third shift.
They've just hung the rafters for the next morality expansion,
I-beams that could tumble from their skyhooks
and reduce this Honda to a schematic for what's gone wrong
somewhere else. So join the realtors' chant: *Location, location, location*
even as ours keeps changing, clutch-pop
and engine throttle. Back on the farm
my horse dreams that he's a horse sleeping, but about to wake.
Presently he will. Sweet affliction! Sweet involute self.
If I say *I think you'll like this book* because I liked it,
what I really mean is *Maybe, just maybe you'll turn out to be me,*
in which case I'll chuck this scratchy voice
and together we'll get down to the business at hand, namely
trading the contents of our back pockets—
recipes, creased baseball cards, gum wrappers, spare change.
I'll drive a hard bargain, but you'll know that, of course;
you'll be prepared. Then the sun's trowel flattens everything to what's
    seemly,
all boxtop syntheses, crucifixion of this urban grid.
I'll put away my wax and needles.
I'll buy a map, you'll idle in the drop-off zone
while I lug my spectrometers and stethoscopes from the hatchback
in their heavy cases. Around us embassies hoist the flags of small countries.
It's like crying at a funeral: do you force the tear or admit what you
    don't feel?

This town's my black opal, I'm your ticket to drive.
In the future let's wear grass skirts so we can tell who's discovered whom.
A moment of silence then: All hail the boustrophedon!
I've set aside a dereliction in the Anacostia of my heart—
six months now and I have yet to let you go.

IN DEFENSE OF ST. PATRICK

Strange to see the angel here, participate, no mistaking that chill for
 the almost intangible application

Of moisture to the transverse cones the jack pines make at regular
 intervals

Beneath the axis of our genuflection. How easy to mistake diligence
 for endeavor, therefore service, the severed hand

In which Titian placed his own end, the pigment; runic, and the
 disease that carried him

Beyond mere questions of title. Think about it: when the sun sets

You can lay claim to any shade the mind binds with the libel of
 color, no one will stop you, no one

Will question you out past the singular hour when sleep raises its
 blurred flag, when even the small factories the needles make

Shut down, rest their tropic cells as far from diminishment as the
 accumulation of unrealized kindness is

From charity despite shared motion. One recommends: appointment
 of an administrator in due course. His report,

Almost decorous as to statements of value, replevy, accounts current

And the figure of a woman left incomplete except for green cloak
 flaring. Body of a child in the parlor, body

Of that which had been Child nacreous, a spectral sheen. God knows
 all deaths collude toward a singularity

Through which time extrapolates, Yeats's gyre no less for pulse-
    prompt

Or the heart's metric. *Sake:* from Old English, dispute, fault, hence
    a purpose,

Advantage, real benefit; litigious root. The paronymy we supposed
    in fact brute dispossession. On a quiet street

The thief's mark moves easily through a succession of broad days,
    whistling, receiving the poor in his mild manner, paying
    careful attention to horticulture but not understanding

How three voices will soon claim that melody. *What, could ye not
    watch with me;*

A touch would have sufficed. Cold flake against forearm. By which
    we are known—

And the fields filling now as those woods did with that wonder.

ZEUGMA

It's easy to love the surfaces of things:
a woman's eyelid, porcelain, the faintly
corrugated silk of a tulip's petal;
to live otherwise is difficult
in this present world. All our affectations
to depth and meaning are contrary
to the more manifest gospel of the skin.
In our dailiness we so often mistake this
for truth, though really it's only
tautology, syllogism at best. The good news
when the sun rises in the morning
is that the sun rises in the morning.
The good news when I write this poem
is that I write it and, in writing, picture
you, perhaps in the same way
Clausewitz's shopgirl pictured him,
every face of her dreaming. *I have decided*
that you are a kind man, she wrote
in the end. *Do not try to find me.*
Nietzsche notwithstanding, the abyss
has become a tourist attraction,
all those ecstatic half-lidded eyes
tilted downward into velvet darkness,
longing for what neither heart
nor hand can touch: which is nothing:
which, if you like, is the koan,
the mad riddle behind love's attraction.
The good news of the sunflower,
the good news of the bristlecone pine—
tropism for survival's sake. Touch by touch

we apprehend our fates, as Oedipus knew.
Piece by piece the world is restored,
this time through the eyes of the dreamer
rather than the reassuring dream.

ALL NIGHT, ALL NIGHT, ALL MORNING

No routine compensates for this dumb hour, the pane streaked and all
    manner of intransigence

Poised, ready to commit at day. I fold my hands and wait for the
    reconnaissance, its green twig, flesh

Against scaled claw in defiance of gravity, wanting to feel that lightness
    lacing and unlacing,

Exchanging the orthogonal for the parallel. Fidelity mothers a good
    deal else

Besides ritual stutter, the page's analogue to its own break: implying
    a motion: a propulsive vector

Travelling wary on forged papers. The border drops away, childhood
    flensed in the glare of a bare bulb.

You said if I'd strip back the eponymous layers I'd become emperor
    over a fluid kingdom—

You promised me that buoyancy. Now my hands are cranes in the
    first light, fine-boned for a man's,

Astonished. Iridescent. Let need be our covenant in common salt,
    after the mercy's gone.

BLAZON

As far as darkness is from God
the world keeps dreaming. I dream with it,
with each breath I consent
to the torsion of these orchards, this fertile plain.
Ahead of me, in the track,
a crow pinches life from an angleworm—
thus answers aftermath with inclusion.
Indeed I covet the storm's violence.
For who among men has overtaken that ragged figure at field's edge?
Consider the waltz, its irresponsible geometry,
replay of the drama
in which teeth strike crisp flesh
at the onset of winter.
This was the ambition of the bud's fluted glory.
This is the superscription of an immoderate regret.
I am that spark, with each return
I lift the image of my conscious flaw
past the pleasure of pure apprehension,
taste, sight, smell, touch,
the whole governing entablature.
Only the ear is vital, only the cochlea preserves its garland.
I walk among the trunks and their ash-collars.
A flame, thus kindled, draws straw
deep from the stone of finished brick, teasing out that thread—
as a stream divides each rush from his long brother
I sift, I harvest, I burn.

NOTES

"Against the Madness of Crowds": In addition to Christopher Smart, the poem quotes Charles Simic in line 11 and Pierre Martory (transl. Ashbery) in line 25.

"Syrinx": The poem is, in part, a refutation of Augustine's contention that the stuff of this world pours forth from God in a double way, intellectually into the minds of the angels and physically into the world of things. The italicized quote in the eighth strophe is from Simone Weil.

"[in the barrow of a forgotten king]": The boy, the orchid, and the piano are nods to C. D. Wright's early poem "Tours."

"In the Gate of Samaria": Ira Sankey (1840–1908) was the singing partner of Dwight L. Moody, nineteenth-century America's best-known Protestant revivalist. Philip P. Bliss (1838–1876), a leading American hymn-writer and Gospel singer of the same period, was also associated with Moody.

"Prophecy: Visitation": I am indebted to *The Visitation*, a painting by Gretchen O. Troibner, as well as to the cloud photographs of Sharon Harper.

"Noli Me Tangere": Virginia Dare (b. 1587) was touted, in earlier American pedagogies, as "the first white child born in North America." She disappeared with her parents and the rest of Sir Walter Raleigh's Roanoke colony in 1591. Various theories have suggested that the Lost Colonists perished from hunger, or at the hands of hostile Indians, or were taken prisoner by those same Indians, or joined them voluntarily. A commemorative stamp in honor of Dare's birth was issued by the U.S. Postal Service in 1937.

"Goldbeater's Skin": Goldbeater's skin was a peculiar kind of security paper perfected in nineteenth-century Europe: The inked image was applied in reverse between a layer of tough, translucent paper and a layer of glue, so that the image, affixed, appeared through the surface of the paper; any attempt to remove it resulted in its destruction. The hidden egg and battlement walls in the last stanza refer to the medieval legend that Naples would always resist would-be conquerors so long as the egg's true location in the eponymous Castel dell'Ovo remained secret.

"Luminous Bodies": The poem quotes or paraphrases Plato, Epicurus, Empedocles, Aristotle, and Galen in turn. I am indebted to David C. Lindberg's *Theories of Vision from Al-Kindi to Kepler* (University of Chicago Press, 1976).

"The Miracles of St. Sebastian": The paintings, and some of the anecdotes, refer to California artist Peter Zokosky (www.zokosky.com).

"Synderesis": or *synteresis*, from Greek via Latin, a guarding or to guard closely. Used by Jerome (347–420) and subsequent scholastic philosophers to denote an innate, as opposed to acquired, knowledge of the basic principles of morality, and in medieval Christian mysticism to refer to the essence of the soul that unites with God.

"Columbus Circle": In Washington, D.C.

"In Defense of St. Patrick": The poem was inspired by the works of contemporary American composer Sara Doncaster, whose text settings include the medieval lyric known as "St. Patrick's Breastplate" as well as William Butler Yeats's "Supernatural Songs." The Titian painting is his *Pietà*, left unfinished at the artist's death in 1576.